Learning to Read, Step by Step!

Ready to Read   Preschool–Kindergarten
• big type and easy words • rhyme and rhythm • picture clues
For children who know the alphabet and are eager to begin reading.

Reading with Help   Preschool–Grade 1
• basic vocabulary • short sentences • simple stories
For children who recognize familiar words and sound out new words with help.

Reading on Your Own   Grades 1–3
• engaging characters • easy-to-follow plots • popular topics
For children who are ready to read on their own.

Reading Paragraphs   Grades 2–3
• challenging vocabulary • short paragraphs • exciting stories
For newly independent readers who read simple sentences with confidence.

Ready for Chapters   Grades 2–4
• chapters • longer paragraphs • full-color art
For children who want to take the plunge into chapter books but still like colorful pictures.

STEP INTO READING® is designed to give every child a successful reading experience. The grade levels are only guides; children will progress through the steps at their own speed, developing confidence in their reading. The F&P Text Level on the back cover serves as another tool to help you choose the right book for your child.

Remember, a lifetime love of reading starts with a single step!

*To the members of International Union of
Operating Engineers Local 478, who build
most of our roads, bridges, and buildings
—M.J.D.*

Acknowledgments: Thanks to Mario Smith, president of Waters Construction; Don Shubert, president of the Connecticut Construction Industries Association; and Michael Riley, president of the Motor Transport Association of Connecticut, who all provided a wealth of contacts. Thanks also to Ray Oneglia and Bob Nardi of O&G Industries and Will Johnson of Walsh Construction, who provided access to their job sites; Ric Suzio of Suzio York Hill, who gave me access to their quarries and concrete plants; Bob Hamilton and the team at Bozzuto's, who let me go for my first truck ride with driver Kyle Chapman; Dorrance Johnson of beyondthefireline.com; Julie Stamper for access to the John Deere archive; bee farmer Rollie Hannan Jr., and his brother Chris, of Honey Meadows Farm; Andy Anastasio and Matthew Goodkin of the Anastasio Group; James Hennessey of Stamford Wrecking; Michael Gates, a tower crane operator with the best view of all; John Woodbury of Gabrielli Truck Sales, who allowed me to pose some trucks; and Christopher Cozzi, Glenn Carrezola, and Britain Szestakow of the Local 478, Operating Engineers, who checked the book for errors. Most of all, thanks to Heidi Kilgras, Anna Membrino, and Jason Zamajtuk of Random House for their support on this project.

Photograph credits: Cover photograph courtesy of Desku Group Inc., copyright © 2015 by Fotolia/photographed by Dmytro Nikitin; pp. 3, 4–5: Dreamstime; pp. 12–13: imac/Alamy; p. 16: Flickr (All rights reserved by granitefan713); p. 20: Flickr (Some rights reserved by Chafer Machinery); p. 21: courtesy of John Deere, Incorporated; pp. 22–23: courtesy of CLAAS; pp. 28–29: beyondthefireline.com; pp. 46–47: Flickr (Some rights reserved by Damian Gadal); p. 48: Flickr (Some rights reserved by haljackey)

Visit us on the Web!
StepIntoReading.com
randomhousekids.com
Educators and librarians, for a variety of teaching tools, visit us at RHTeachersLibrarians.com

Library of Congress Cataloging-in-Publication Data is available upon request.
ISBN 978-0-553-51240-3 (pbk.) — ISBN 978-0-553-51241-0 (lib. bdg.) —
ISBN 978-0-307-55666-0 (ebook)

Printed in the United States of America
10 9 8 7 6 5 4 3 2 1
This book has been officially leveled by using the F&P Text Level Gradient™ Leveling System.

Random House Children's Books supports the First Amendment and celebrates the right to read.

STEP
3
READING ON YOUR OWN

STEP INTO READING®

A NON-FICTION READER

HEAVY-DUTY TRUCKS

by Joyce Milton

photographs by Michael J. Doolittle

Random House 🏠 New York

On a busy highway,

huge trucks

go whizzing by.

What would it be like

to drive a really big truck?

Truckers shift gears a lot.
Big trucks have ten gears—
or more!

Truckers talk to other drivers on
their CB radios.

Sometimes they
even sleep in their trucks.
Many big trucks have a bed
behind the driver's seat.
Truckers call this bed
the *sleeping box*.

There are two kinds of
trucks on the road.
Some trucks are all
in one piece.
They are called *straight trucks*.

But the biggest trucks
have two parts.
They are called
tractor-trailers.
The driver sits
in the *tractor,*
or cab.
Cargo goes in back,
in the *trailer.*

Some trailers have
eight wheels in back
and none at all in front.
They are called *semi-trailers,*
or *semis,* for short.
The front of the semi
rests on metal legs.

The truck driver

hooks the semi to his cab.

Then he raises the legs.

Now he is ready

to hit the road.

Tractor-trailers can haul

almost anything.

There is room
inside this moving truck
for a whole houseful
of furniture.

Open-bed trailers
are trailers with open sides.
They carry the heaviest loads.
Brand-new cars
can ride piggyback
on an *auto hauler*.

These telephone poles are
now ready to be placed
in the ground.

Some trailers are
huge refrigerators on wheels.
Truckers call them *reefers*.

Reefers carry meat,

frozen foods,

and even candy bars.

Other trucks carry
live animals—horses, cattle,
or sometimes bees!
This loader is moving
crates of bees onto
a flatbed straight truck.

The beekeeper usually
moves the bees at
dawn or dusk,
because they are less active
when it is cool.

A *tractor* is an important
truck for a farmer.
It pulls machines
that help work the fields.

One machine plants corn.

Another picks the corn

when it is ripe.

Inside the tractor's cab
there is a computer
that runs the planter.
The farmer can use
the Internet to listen to music
while he picks the corn.

Cities need big trucks, too.
The *street sweeper* is like
a giant broom on wheels.

Garbage trucks carry away trash—tons of it!

These trucks are called
cherry pickers.
Are they used for
picking cherries?
No!
These workers need to fix
a broken power line.
The cherry pickers
take them up, up, up
into the air.

Firefighters arrive
at a burning building.
The *pumper trucks*
pump water from
a fire hydrant.

These *ladder trucks*

carry ladders

tall enough to reach

a fifth-story window.

There's a new building
going up in town.
Here's your chance
to see some special
heavy-duty trucks.

The *bulldozer*

is the first to go to work.

It pushes heavy rocks

and piles of dirt

out of the way.

Backhoes dig holes.
The scoop on the back end
of the backhoe
is called a *bucket*.
The bucket can hold
almost a ton of dirt.

This giant backhoe
is called an *excavator*.
It has tracks instead
of wheels.
The tracks keep it from
sinking into mud.
Excavators can dig
very deep holes.

Excavators can do
other tough jobs, too.
This excavator uses
a *grapple* to demolish
a building,
piece by piece.

A *rock hammer*
is attached to this
excavator.
The rock hammer
can break up huge
pieces of concrete.

Carrying away

tons of dirt

is a job for a monster

dump truck.

This one's wheels
are eight feet high—
that's a lot taller than
a grown man!
The driver has to use a ladder
to get to his seat.

Cranes are the weight lifters
of the truck family.
The crane's long arm
lifts steel beams
high into the air.
Driving a crane
can be dangerous.
One mistake,
and the crane
can tip right over.

The tallest cranes
are called *tower cranes*.
This tower crane
is eight stories tall.

Before a road is repaved,
a *milling machine* has to
tear up the old asphalt.
This milling machine
grinds up old pavement
and shoots it into a truck.

It can be used to make
brand-new pavement.

A *concrete mixer*
is like a giant blender.
The drum turns
to mix the concrete.
Then it pours it out
onto the roadbed.

Another truck, called
a *screed asphalt paver,*
spreads new pavement
across the road.

Soon the highway

will be filled with cars.

And trucks, too—

lots of them.

Trucks keeping our
store shelves
filled with good things.
Trucks doing all kinds
of heavy-duty jobs.

The next time
you take a ride,
look out the window.
How many heavy-duty
trucks can you name?